D1407835

Other giftbooks by Exley:
The Fanatics Guide to Cats
Glorious Cats
Kittens!
Cat Lovers Address Book

Published simultaneously in 1997 by Exley Publications in Great Britain, and Exley Giftbooks in the USA.

12   11   10   9   8   7   6   5   4   3   2   1

Cartoons and text copyright © Roland Fiddy 1997
Copyright © Exley Publications Ltd 1997

ISBN 1-85015-850-9

Edited by Helen Exley.
Cartoons and text by Roland Fiddy.
Designed by Pinpoint.
Printed in Dubai.

Exley Publications Ltd, 16 Chalk Hill, Watford, Herts WD1 4BN UK.
Exley Giftbooks, 232 Madison Avenue, Suite 1206, NY 10016, USA.

If it's Cute and Crazy, it must be My Cat!

PURR
PURR
PURR

Cartoons by Roland Fiddy

EXLEY
NEW YORK · WATFORD, UK

Cast out Cat

Cantankerous Cat

Cunning Cat

Cute Cat

Criminal Cat

A Comical Cat

Fat Cat

Cosseted Cat

Conceited Cat

Contentment

Celebration!

Caution

Fury

Conical Cat

Corpulent
Cats

Alley Cat

Courageous Cat

Confrontationa

Cats

Two Complacent Cats

Cuddly Cats

Caterwauling Cats

Crazy Cat

Tired Tom

Tough Tom

Pitiful Puss

Scaredy Cat

Psychic Cat

Contemplative
Cat